How to Make REAL MONEY Online

A Step by Step guide to Making Money Online

First Edition
2020

BY MPUMELELO MESLANE

ISBN: 9798654190918

eBook Edition
Published for Worldwide Distribution

Note from the Author

HOW TO MAKE **REAL** MONEY ONLINE is a step by step, practical guide on how to make real money online using a computer or mobile phone and a reliable internet connection. These methods of making money are freely available worldwide.

This eBook aims to share some of the simplest, most practical and proven ways on how to make money starting today. Results are dependent on your actions, dedication and commitment into applying these money-making formulas correctly.

All these money-making formulas have been proven and they do indeed work. I have personally tried them myself and made a steady flow of monthly income online.

Acknowledgement

The Author wishes to acknowledge and thank all the companies referenced in this eBook. This eBook supports the growth of their businesses and the role they play in creating global income online. This eBook aims to reduce global unemployment and create a new wave of global online entrepreneurs.

Table Contents

1. Online Marketing Research & Testing

Are your tired of your daily 9 to 5 job and have been searching online for real, simple and flexible ways of making real money online?

I am sure you have you googled rigorously for ways to make money online and your search results was just too overwhelming for you. And you also didn't know where to start or how to execute some of the online money-making steps.

Well, rest assured, I am here to provide you with a practical, easy way to make money online. Let us start with the Online Marketing Research & Testing companies that offer you flexible and easy ways of making money online. Most of these companies pay you via PayPal. Let's begin.

I. Let me start with the first one, **Appen,** **(www.appen.com):**

Appen is always seeking candidates in different countries and languages for online work-from-home opportunities range from simple tasks that can be completed in less than one hour to on-going projects that last for months or longer.

To apply, please follow the next steps:

Type on your web browser: **http://www.appen.com**

The click on "**Jobs**" tab

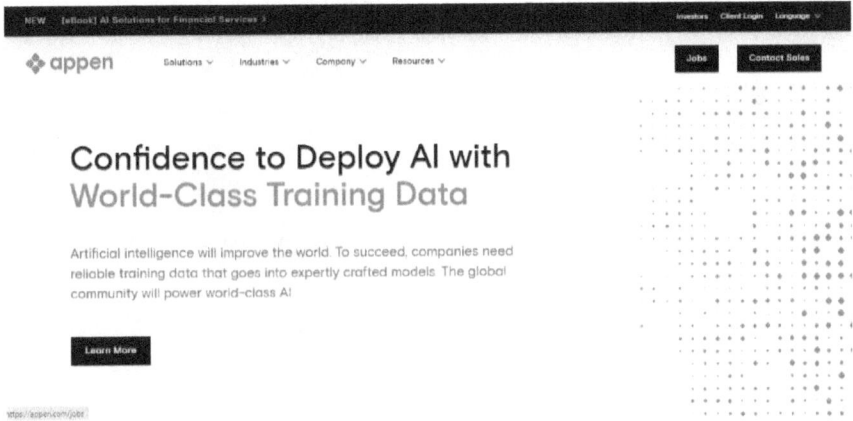

Then you will be taken to a page called – Part-time Flexible, whereby you click on "**Apply**" for the desired job. Ranging from Projects, Micro Tasks to Surveys & Data Collection. Complete the registration form. Your application will be screened before you become eligible for the online job.

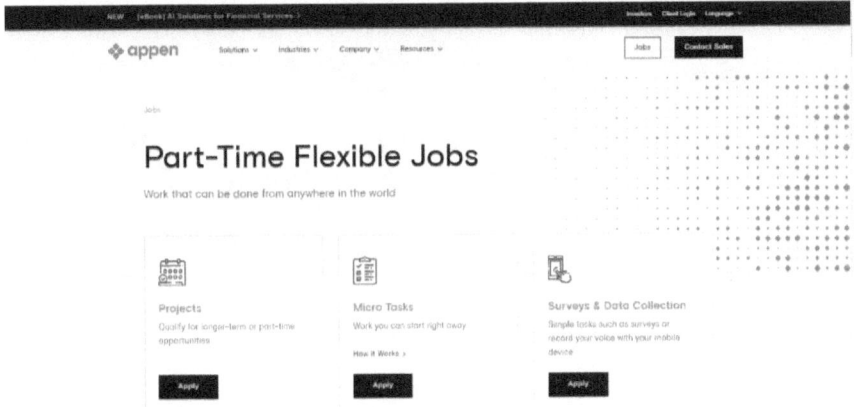

Once you are eligible to participate, Appen team will send you a link to a Project Page that lists the projects available to you in your country and/or your language. There are always new and exciting projects being added so visit their web page often. You must also open an Account with **Payoneer** (www.payoneer.com) to receive money from Appen.

Some of the Appen **opportunities** that may be available:

- Search Media Evaluation (Work with the world's top search engine companies)

- Social Media Evaluation (Help improve social media around the globe)

- Translation

- Transcription

- Survey and Data Collection (Short projects that last from 15 minutes to three hours)

- Linguistic Specialties (Text to Speech, Computational, Phonetics, Pronunciation, Annotation, etc.)

- Lexicon Annotation

- Speech Evaluation

II.   Next online marketing research company is called **uTest.com (www.utest.com).** uTest by Applause is the number one platform for freelance software testing and feedback.

All you need to do is visit **www.utest.com** and click on "**Sign up**"

Complete the registration form to apply.

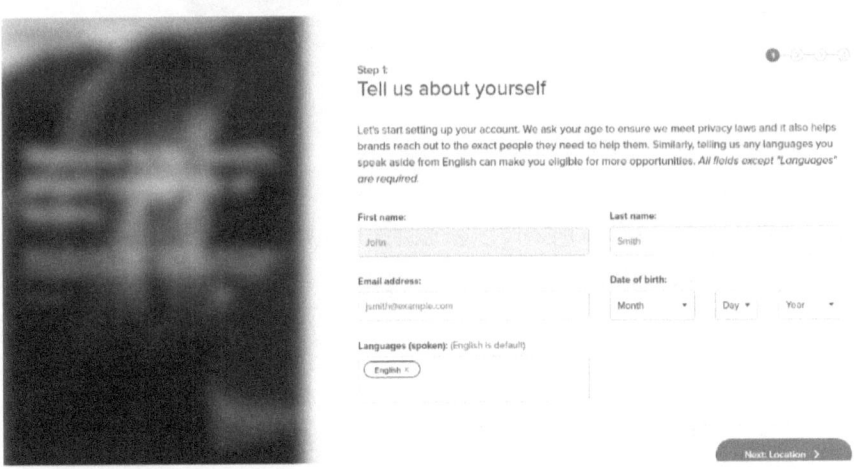

You will receive a confirmation email after registration.

III. The third online testing platform is **Userlytics (www.userlytics.com)**.

You will be user testing websites, prototypes, advertisements, videos and other types of material from small start-up companies to those of large well-known corporations. You will NOT be asked to view sites that do not meet their Terms of Use guidelines. You can contact them before beginning a user experience test if you have doubts about its content.

To **apply**, click on **"tester sign up"** and enter your email address.

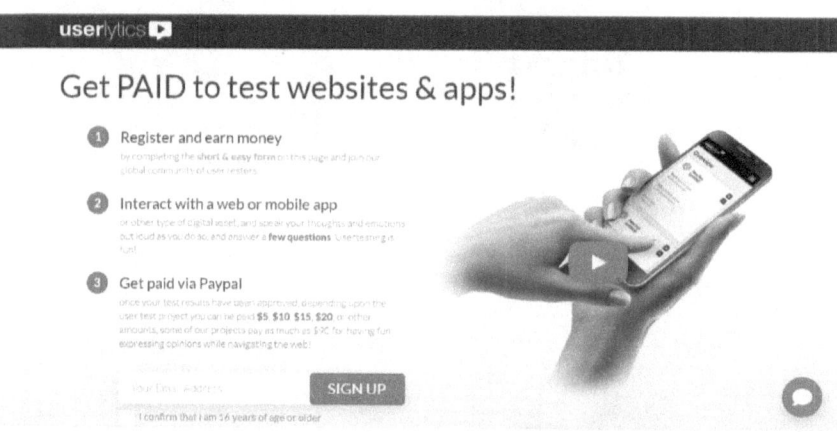

Afterwards, you will receive a confirmation email with link. Click on the link to complete the registration process.

IV. The fourth online testing platform is **Validately (www.validately.com)**.

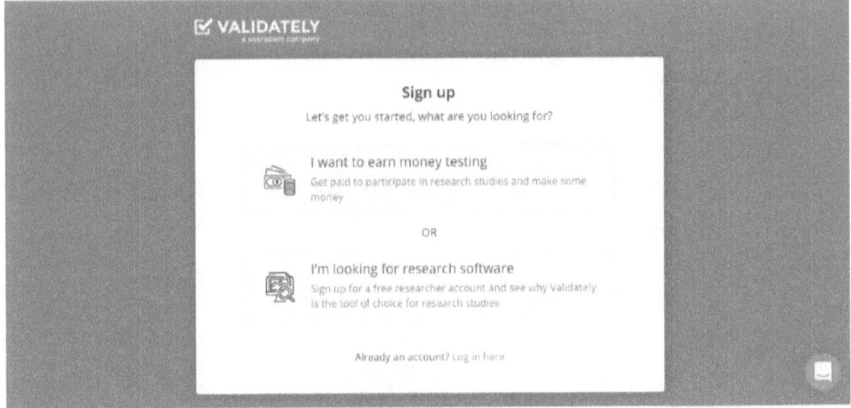

Visit the **www.validately.com** and click on "**Sign up**".   Next, click on "I want to earn money testing"

Then click on "**Create Account**"

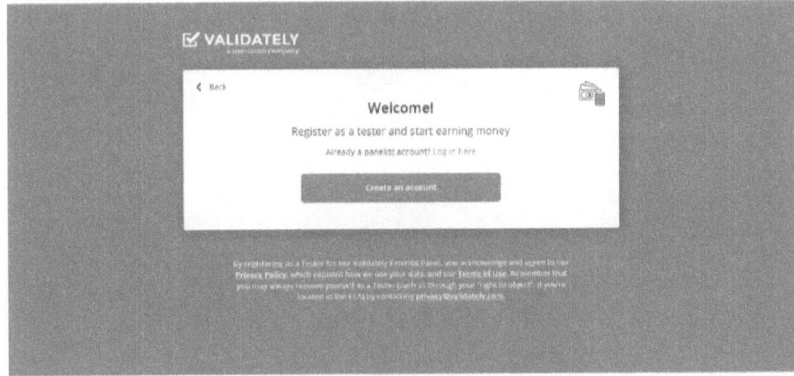

Thereafter, you will answer 16 questions to qualify. Once you have completed the qualifying questions, you will receive an email confirming that your application will be reviewed.

☑ VALIDATELY

Question 1

What type of mobile device do you own?

Select as many as you like.

iPhone

iPad

Android

Other

Next

FAQ Sign up Login Terms Privacy

Once you receive the confirmation email, just be patient while they assess your application form.

Notes:

One thing to remember with Online Marketing Research & Testing jobs, you must be committed and dedicate at least 1 to 2 hours daily depending on the task time required. Create a PayPal account (www.paypal.com) to receive payments from these companies.

2. Become an Affiliate Marketer

Affiliate marketing is the process of earning a commission by promoting other people's (or company's) products. You find a product you like, promote it to others and earn a piece of the profit for each sale that you make.

An **Affiliate Marketer** is the person who promotes other people's products in return for a commission from a successful sale. An Affiliate Marketer promotes other people's products using their unique promotional link that has been assigned to them which you can insert it in their blogs, websites, social media and email signatures etc. The aim is to drive huge web traffic to the link and create a successful sale.

There are a number of affiliate programs out there, each with its own niche of products and commission structure.

The most popular affiliate platform which caters for a variety of product niches, is platform called **ClickBank** **(www.clickbank.com).**

For the purpose of this eBook, we shall focus on ClickBank because they are a leading global retailer with their own affiliate marketplace.

First step is to visit **www.clickbank.com** and then click on **"Sign Up"**

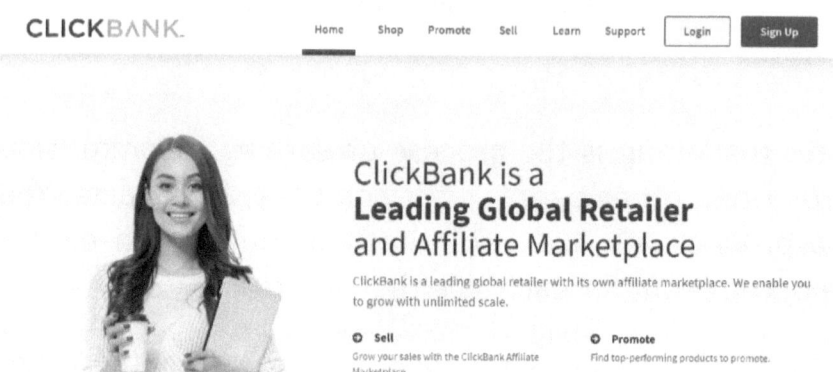

Then complete the registration form,

Once you have completed the registration form, you will receive a confirmation email.

Once your account is active, you will be able to **"Sign In"**. The first screen to be displayed will be your dashboard as per image in the next page:

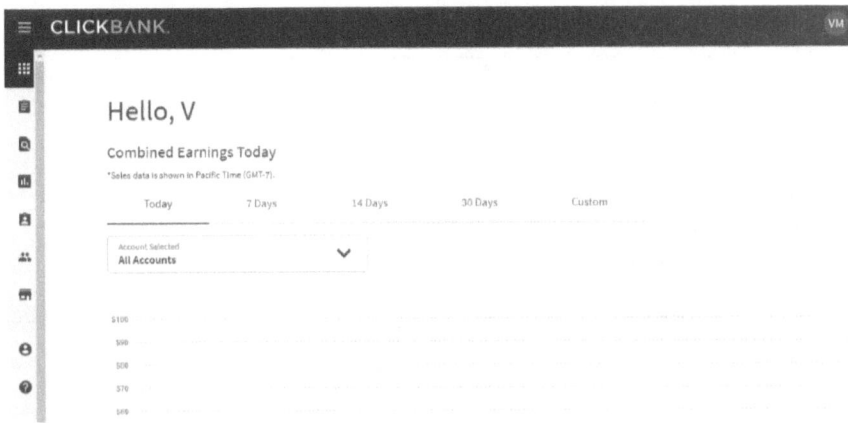

Your dashboard shows your combined earnings for the last 24 hours to 30 days and beyond.

Then click on the "Marketplace" icon that resembles a shop icon. The following **Marketplace** screen should open on a new website tab:

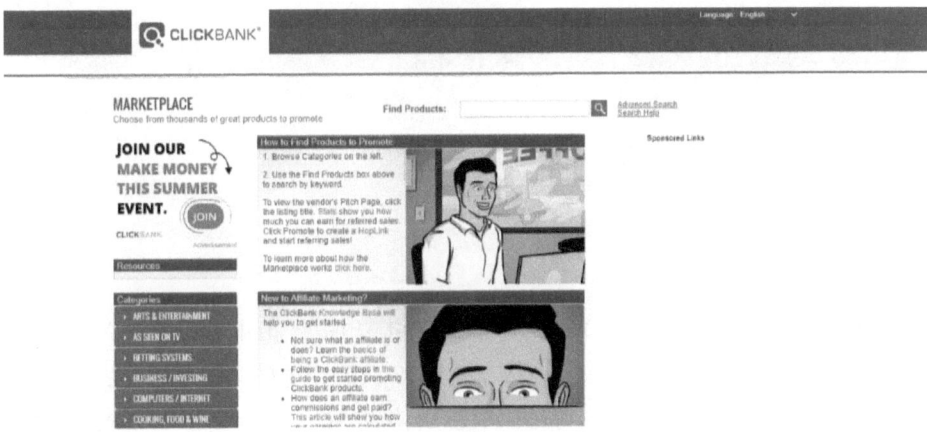

Now you have a choice of choosing your favorite niche ranging from Arts & Entertainment to Travel. When you click on your favorite niche, you will choose from number of great products to promote under that niche as per next image:

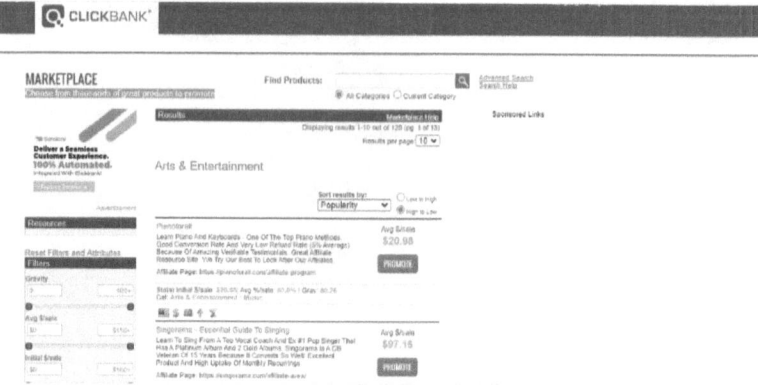

You will then see the various average commission payment for each product affiliate. Once you have chosen the product affiliate with the best commission, click on the icon named "PROMOTE". Then enter your account nickname and click on "GENERATE HOPLINKS". An affiliate link will be generated which you will click on the end of the link to copy it.

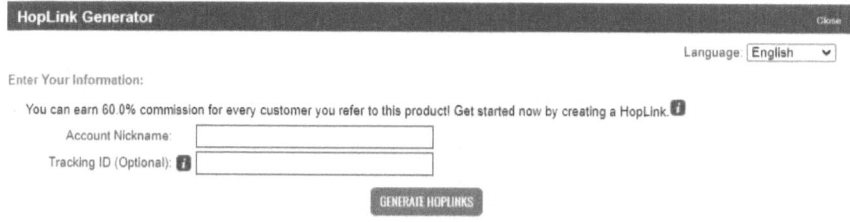

Now that you have the ClickBank affiliate link of the product you want to promote. Visit **www.cuttly.com** to shorten your affiliate link URL. This website will also help you count and monitor traffic to your affiliate link. Now, the next steps are to drive traffic to that affiliate link. You can use the following methods:

a. **Social Media** – Join online groups (with lots of members) that relate to your affiliate ClickBank product niche and share your link with the group. Importantly, do just share in form of spam but share more information about the product niche and what the group will benefit by clicking on your link. Also include international trending #hashtags when posting your affiliate ClickBank product link on social media. This will drive more traffic to your link.

b. Next, you can create a **YouTube video** about your product niche and add your affiliate ClickBank link in your video description. Don't forget to include video tags about your product niche when uploading the video to YouTube.

c. Place your product affiliate link your **email signature** and also your **"out of office" notification** so that whenever you send out an email, your link is distributed to all your recipients and vice-versa, when they send you an email, your out-office has the affiliate link.

Note:

*Importantly, **do not spam** people with your affiliate link unnecessary. Please note some social media accounts may block affiliate links. Use your discretion when posting affiliate links.*

3. Audio Transcription Freelancers

Audio transcription is the process of converting speech from an audio file into written text. This can be any recording featuring audio - an interview recording, academic research, a video clip etc.

Audio Transcription Freelancer is someone that transcribes audio into written text for a client or a company as a freelancer.

Transcription can be learnt easily and most of the companies can hire transcribers that are new to the industry without any formal qualification, but most importantly specialize in grammar and language.

One of the best websites for Audio Transcription Freelancers is **Rev.com (www.rev.com).**

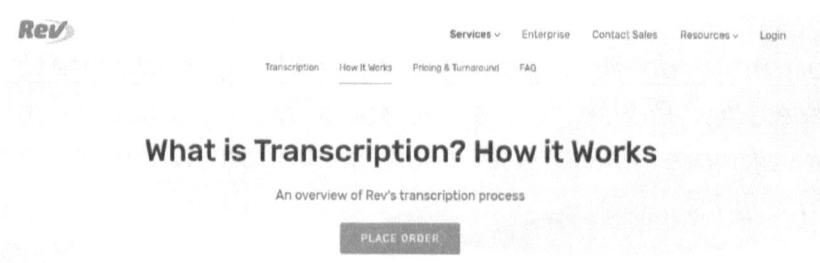

Visit the website **www.rev.com** and on the main page, scroll to the bottom to the freelancer's link.

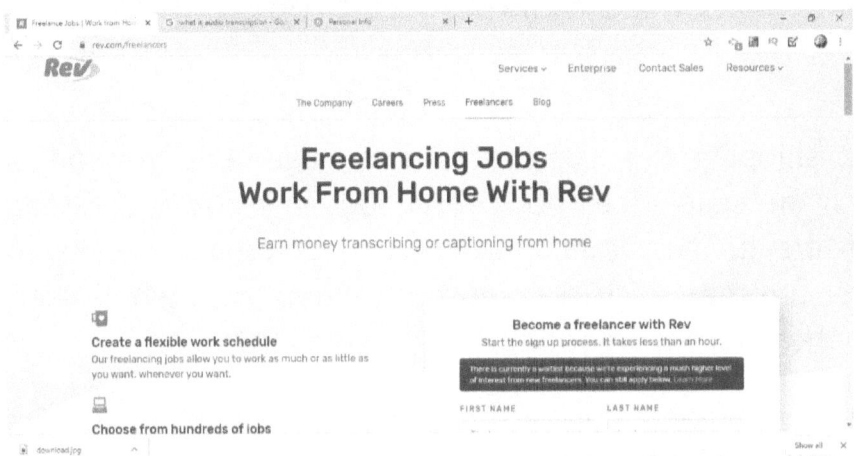

Then fill in your personal details under the "Become a freelancer with Rev" and click "Next". You will then be required to do a grammar and transcription assessment to qualify for the transcription job – there is no time limit. Once you submit your assessment, you will receive a confirmation email stating that your application is being reviewed.

Once approved, you will then be able to choose your transcription jobs available to you. You can be paid anything from **$0.30 to $1.10 per audio/video minute**.

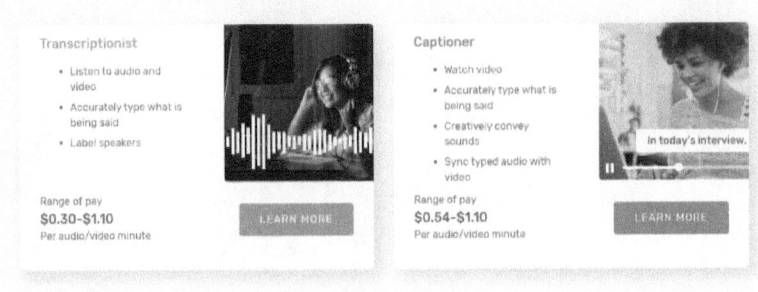

4. Online Market Place Drop Shipping

Drop shipping is a supply chain management method in which the seller does not keep goods in stock but instead transfers its customer's orders and shipment details to either the manufacturer, another retailer, or a wholesaler, who then ships the goods directly to the customer.

Best ways of conducting a successful drop-shipping business is to use existing credible largescale manufactures and reputable online marketplace.

First step is to find a profitable product that you want to "drop-ship" to clients. The most credible largescale manufactures are listed on the following websites:

AliExpress: (www.aliexpress.com) Click on "Join"

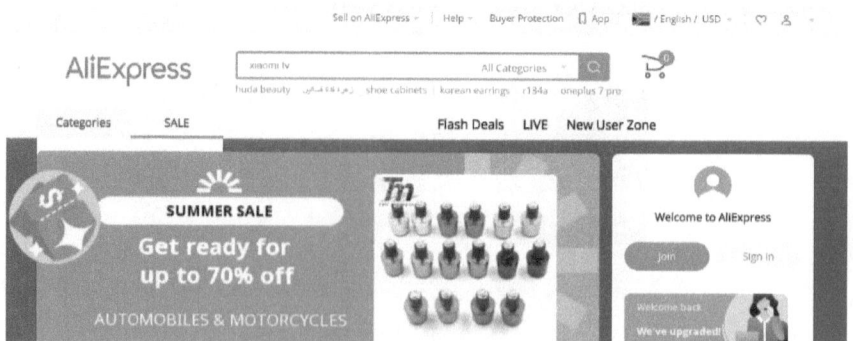

Alibaba (www.alibaba.com) Click on "Join Free"

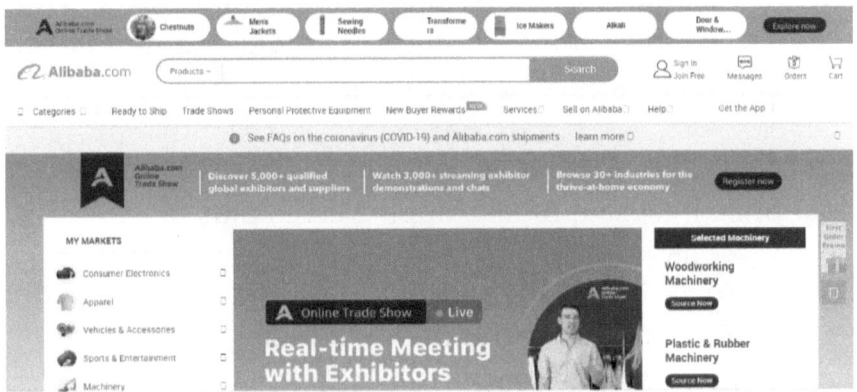

Once you have registered with these online Chinese manufactures, you can search for products you want to sell as drop-shipping order on other online American marketplace such as eBay or Amazon for a profit. Remember to open an **eBay** account **(www.ebay.com)** or Amazon **(www.sellercentral.amazon.com)**

For eBay, you can check out what are the top selling products by visiting the website called **www.watchcount.com**. Here you will be able to see which products are in demand. Once you find your product on Watchcount, then search for it on AliExpress or Alibaba and compare prices with eBay or Amazon. Then list your products on eBay or Amazon marking up your price to include shipping and taxes.

You have 30 days to fulfill orders on eBay once someone buys your product on eBay and the PayPal payment is cleared on your side. Simply visit AliExpress or Alibaba and place an order for the exact, same product but shipping address be addressed to the customer who bought from you on eBay. Once the order is shipped and there is tracking number from AliExpress / Alibaba, simply add it to your eBay order and click shipped on eBay as well. Remember to create a spreadsheet listing of your orders.

Your profit is the difference between AliExpress and eBay product price inclusive of all shipping costs plus taxes.

Drop Shipping is a quantity business, the more you sell, the more you make money without ever keeping stock or using your own money to buy stock.

Other Drop Shipping Way:

Other ways to do drop-shipping business, is to create your own store with **Shopify (www.shopify.com)** where you list your products instead of eBay or Amazon platforms. With Shopify store, there is a monthly fee after the expiry of the 14-day free trial. Benefit with Shopify, you can list as many items compare to eBay or Amazon which is limited. You can customize your own Shopify store to suit your style.

5. Online Video Ad & Courses

One of the best ways to make money online is by uploading videos on **YouTube.** YouTube is accessed by millions and millions of viewers daily.

You can monetize (make money) your YouTube videos once you reach 4000 views (hours) and 1000 subscribers where ads will be displayed on the commencement your videos (also in the middle of the video). Once you reach the monetization requirements, simply open an AdSense account to link it to you YouTube account. The more views the more money you will be paid in Ad revenue (search for Google AdSense on google).

First steps in making money with YouTube, is to find a popular niche, then create a YouTube channel (visit **YouTube Studio**:

https://www.youtube.com/create_channel),

then create a video around the niche e.g. fitness or exercise and then add a ClickBank affiliate link (as explained earlier) to get additional commission above the Ad revenue.

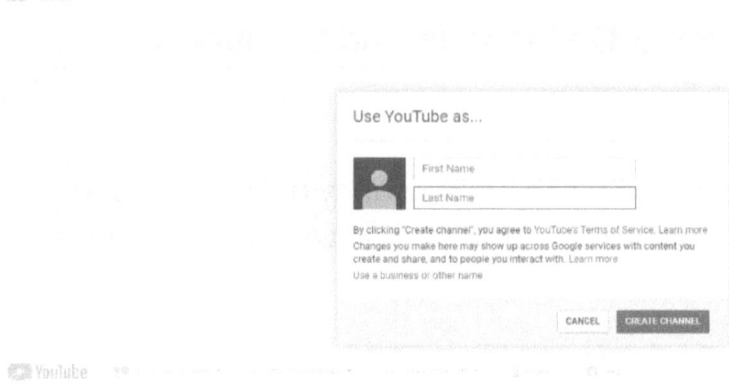

It's important to professionalize your YouTube channel with channel art that is related to your niche.

Next step, visit **Vidiq (www.vidiq)** and add this Vidiq extension to you chrome browser (just click on "Add Extension" on the Vidiq main page). Vidiq will enable you to add popular video tags to your uploaded videos in order to attract more visitors to your videos. Vidiq is also able to monitor your YouTube videos engagement with visitors.

Online Courses:

Another way to make money online, is to register for free courses online **edX (www.edx.org)** and get certified then sell that same skill on **Fiverr.com (www.fiverr.com)** , **People Per Hour (www.peopleperhour.com)**, **Upwork (www.upwork.com)**or create a new course for other people on **Udemy.com (www.udemy.com)** using newly acquired skills.

Millions of people visit Fiverr and Udemy every month that means you can make money from people who are looking for you newly acquired skills.

Udemy is also a great platform to acquire new skills as well. Your can learn anywhere, anytime.

6. On-Demand Production Stores

Another easy way of making money online is to visit the following on-demand product production websites such as **CafePress (www.cafepress.com)** and **Teespring (www.teespring.com)**

CafePress allows you to design your own custom products, from mugs to t-shirts and get paid a commission on the sale of those products. You take of the designing and they take care of the marketing, production, shipping to the customer for Free.

All you have to do is click on "**Join**" on their website and start designing.

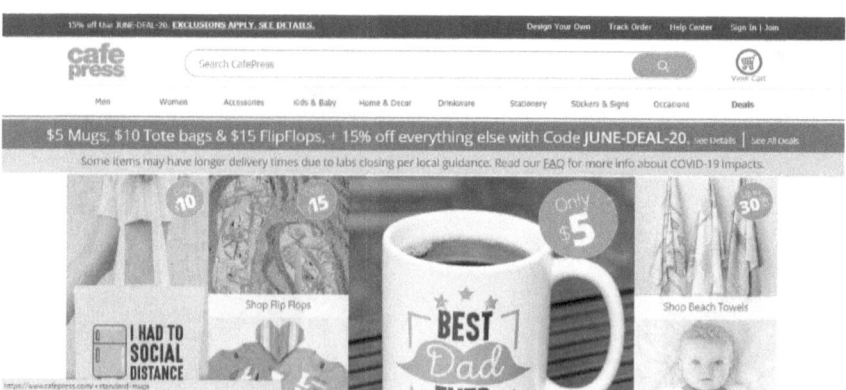

Teespring also allows you to design your own product but they specialize mostly in t-shirts. So, if you have a great design for a t-shirt, you can make money from this website. They also take care of the marketing, production and fulfilment of the order to the customer. You can mock-up your profit on their base price.

Simply click on: "**Get Started**" on their website.

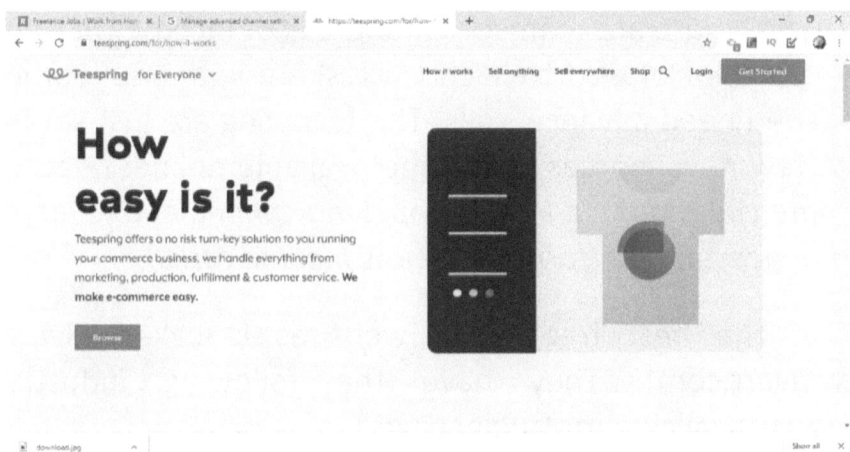

This is another great on-demand e-Commerce business that can bring you passive income.

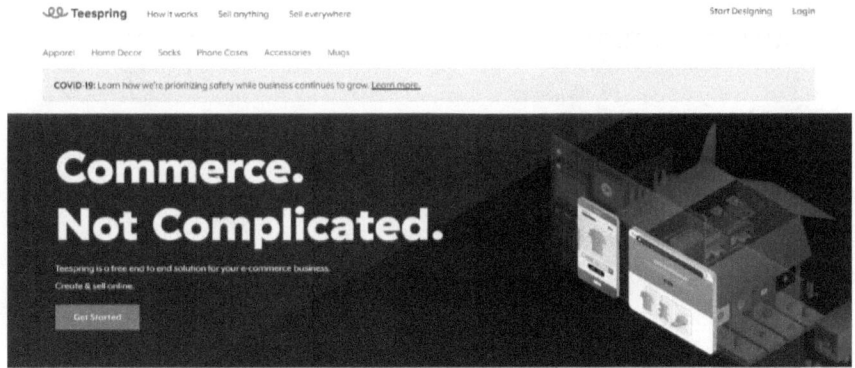

Note: *For the above business to be a success, use design software that is freely available in the internet.*

7. Online Skills Freelancing & Other Tasks

Nowadays, there are many other sources of income that do not require lot of effort which I will share with you. Some don't even need advance skills. The following are just some of the few new sources of income available online: *(Please that note you require a PC/ Laptop, Smartphone and reliable internet access to perform the below income tasks)*

One of the best freelancing websites is called **Fiverr (www.fiverr.com)**. They have the following industry categories available for freelancing:

- Graphic Design

- Music & Audio

- Digital Marketing

- Writing & Translation

- Business

- Programming & Tech

- Video & Animation

If your current skills set that fits into any of the above industry categories, then Fiverr is your freelancing platform.

How It Works

1. Create A Gig

Sign up for free, set up your Gig, and offer your work to our global audience.

2. Deliver Great Work

Get notified when you get an order and use our system to discuss details with customers.

3. Get Paid

Get paid on time, every time. Payment is transferred to you upon order completion.

First steps are to visit **www.fiverr.com** and then click on "**Become Seller**" at the top menu bar.

fiverr Q Find Services [Search] Fiverr Pro English RZAR Become a Seller Sign In [Join]

Graphics & Design   Digital Marketing   Writing & Translation   Video & Animation   Music & Audio   Programming & Tech   Business   Lifestyle   Industries

Popular professional services

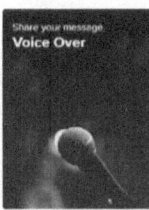

The click on "Become Seller" again in the next page:

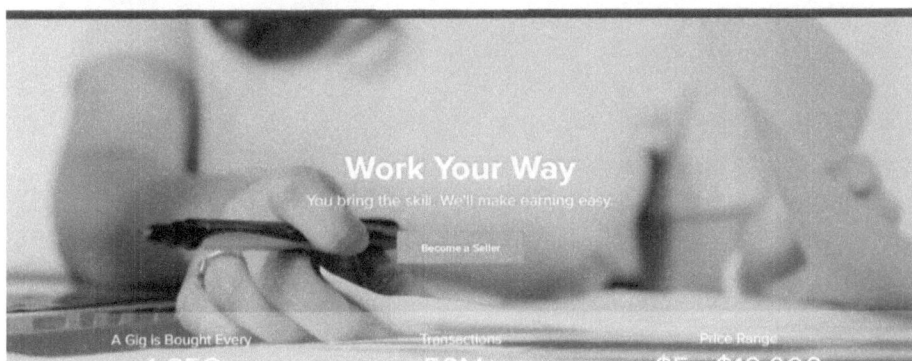

Thereafter, you must create a credible freelancer profile. Remember you are selling your skills in exchange for money.

Once registered, you will get a confirmation email.

Other Skills Freelancing websites:

People Per Hour: www.peopleperhour.com

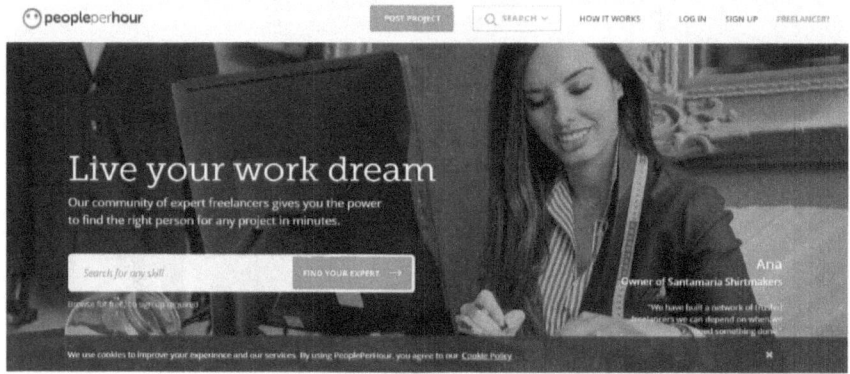

Upwork: www.upwork.com

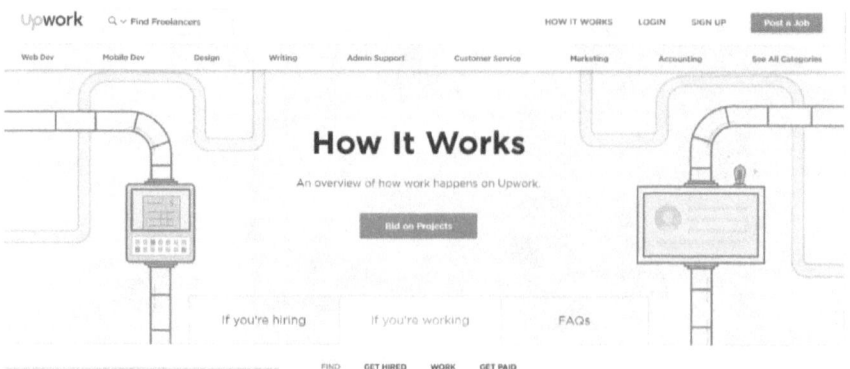

Other Tasks:

Online Freelancing – Create a free website *(www.wix.com)*, advertising your services such plumbing or flight bookings or dog walking or cleaning etc. and then email your website link using email marketing platforms to your family and friends

Mobrog - Online Paid Surveys – Pays up to $1 per survey e.g. www.mobrog.com *(register on their website and they will email you their surveys to complete.)*

Task Rabit - Get paid to complete tasks (*Payment varies upon task completed)* – visit their website for registration *(google Task Rabit)*

VIPKid - Online Tutors and earn up to $22 hour *(google VIPkid). (Country availability may apply)*

WIX - Create a free website at ww.wix.com and add "relevant" web content to it then register with Google AdSense - you will be able to place their Ads links or banners on your website and they will in return pay you per click or impression for anyone clicking on these links. *(Importantly, you must drive good organic visitor traffic to your website). You can also register with Amazon Associates program. (google AdSense and Amazon Associates program)*

Craigslist or Gumtree or OLX – Sell your unwanted goods or services on these websites and get paid.

Social Media Marketer / Influencer – Twitter & Instagram. You will only able to attract sponsors if you have a reasonable high number of followers on these platforms. You can contact related sponsors or companies or brands to advertise on your social media platform depending on your content *(Social Media rules apply)*

GoDaddy Reseller Program – Buy a reseller package starting at +/- $17 per month from GoDaddy.com and resell their domain hosting/website building packages for a commission using their platform. *(This income stream is good if you have additional cash in your bank account for their monthly deductions)*

Online Virtual Assistant – If you are a very organized, meticulous and a professional individual, you can become a VA (like a Personal Assistant) for Company Executives or CEOs. You can book their meetings, flights, executive lunches and more at a fixed daily rate. *(You can create a simple free website from www.wix.com for marketing your services)*

ACX – www.acx.com – Earn money by auditioning for audio books. You can earn either by royalties or flat fee for your work.

Up-load – www.up-load.com – Get paid to upload documents. Simply register on this website.

File-up – www.file-up.org – this site pays you to also upload documents.

Textbroker – www.textbroker.com – make money by writing. Sign-up on their website.

In conclusion:

There are so many ways to make real money from the internet using your computer and a reliable internet connection. For training on the above, simple email me.

"There is an abundance of money in the world"

8. About the Author

The Author — Mpumelelo Meslane

HOW TO MAKE REAL MONEY ONLINE is a step by step practical guide on how to make real money online using your computer or mobile phone. These methods of making money are available worldwide.

About the Author:

Mr. Mpumelelo Meslane is a creative South African author, entrepreneur, blogger, vlogger, marketer born during the harsh era of the "Apartheid" regime, when society was still segregated by race and resources for any young aspiring black authors was limited.

Growing up against these societal blockages, he managed to acquire a college education and a received many top employee accolades from a leading corporate company. He has worked for many corporate industries from construction, e-commerce, shipping to insurance which has diversified his skills and knowledge.

He wrote his first book in 2008 and later published the following books:

- My Noble Motivational Quotes

- The Naked Way to Success

- A Singe Black Men's Guide to Fatherhood

- My Bubblegum Motivational Thoughts

- Secrets Why Some Black Men Cheat

- How to Start Over After Losing Your Job

- How to Make Real Money Online (eBook)

These books are available on the following online platforms:

- Google Books

- Amazon.com

- Exclusive Books (online only)

- Lulu.com

- Kindle

Mr. Mpumelelo Meslane has a passion for writing self-help books, driven by a need to inspire young men and women to become successful in all areas of their lives from family, relationship to career.

He aims to continue writing more self-help books, novels and to become the best-selling international author.

Contact:

Email: **affiliatenow4ever@gmail.com** (for training requests)

Twitter: **@meslane**

THANK YOU FOR YOUR SUPPORT

MESLANE PUBLISHERS

www.ingramcontent.com/pod-product-compliance
Lightning Source LLC
Chambersburg PA
CBHW030550220526
45463CB00007B/3050